MAIN STREET
A portrait of small-town Michigan

by Manny Crisostomo

This book is dedicated to my parents, Herman and Maria Crisostomo, with love.

MAIN STREET
A portrait of small-town Michigan

by Manny Crisostomo

Edited by Marcia Joy Prouse
With an introduction by Thomas BeVier

Detroit Free Press
Historical Society of Michigan
1986

Main Street
A portrait of small-town Michigan

Photography and text: Manny Crisostomo
Picture editing and design: Marcia Joy Prouse
Editing: Kevin Roseborough
Copy editing: Bob Cronin, Kelly Feusse and John Lear
Page production: Carol A. Jaszcz
Publications co-ordinator: Michele Kapecky

Published by the Detroit Free Press
Detroit, Michigan 48231
and
Historical Society of Michigan
Ann Arbor, Michigan 48104

Supported by a grant
to the Historical Society of Michigan
by ANR Pipeline Co.,
a subsidiary of Coastal Corp.

Library of Congress Catalog Card number 86-071513
ISBN 0-937247-00-6

Historical Society of Michigan

Michigan's small towns and villages are often overlooked in the rush of commercial and residential development. Yet they are home to many — an integral element in the fabric of the state. Their people are that fabric's strength. Indeed, their love of country and state is expressed in their love of hometown.

Manny Crisostomo has captured, through his camera lens, the essence of small-town Michigan in this book. "Main Street: A portrait of small-town Michigan," is not only a testimony to these places but to Manny's appreciation of them and their citizens.

The Historical Society of Michigan is honored to co-publish Main Street with the Detroit Free Press. Founded in 1828, the Society is Michigan's statewide, membership-supported organization dedicated to the promotion and publication of the state's history. Many of its thousands of members are residents of small towns and their love of Michigan and its history is only surpassed by their dedication to the history of their own towns.

Appropriately, Main Street appears during the celebration of Michigan's 150th anniversary of statehood — its sesquicentennial — for it praises the people of Michigan, in whose hearts the event will be truly honored. The society thanks the Detroit Free Press for inaugurating the "Main Street Michigan" photo series in 1984. Its support of it since then, culminating in the production of this book, is a most appropriate sesquicentennial gift to the State of Michigan.

The involvement of the Historical Society of Michigan in this publication would have not been possible without the financial assistance of the ANR Pipeline Co. of Detroit. We deeply appreciate the interest and support expressed by its representatives throughout the entire project.

The Historical Society of Michigan is pleased to dedicate this book to the people of Michigan and to make it available for the enjoyment of people everywhere, in big cities and small towns.

— *Thomas L. Jones,*
Executive Director
Historical Society of Michigan

5

MICHIGAN SESQUICENTENNIAL
1837 · 1987

Detroit Free Press

HISTORICAL SOCIETY OF MICHIGAN · 1874

ANR Pipeline Company

a subsidiary of The Coastal Corporation

6

Contents

On the cover: Phyllis and George Lafkas stand in front of their 1958 Plymouth Belvedere, which has 41,000 miles on it. The car is parked in front of Negaunee's Olympia Bar, which George Lafkas' father used to own.

Acknowledgments

I would like to gratefully acknowledge the following:

The small towners who lent me their time, faces, moments and warm hospitality.

A group of outstate Michiganders who supported me with ideas, use of their darkrooms, directions and home-cooked meals — Richard and Nancy Anderson, Don Pavloski, Bill Rabe, John Russell, Charlie Espach, Rex Larson, Chris Miller, Scott Harmsen, Nelson Yonder, Lisa Lee and Amy Thorpe.

The editors at the Detroit Free Press for believing in the Main Street Michigan series and to Tom Jones and members of the Historical Society of Michigan for believing in the book.

For technical and moral support the following: Randy Miller, Sandy White, Tony Spina, Miki Graznak and the Free Press photo staff.

Keith Piaseczny of the Urban Center of Photography for making the prints in this book.

My inspirational cheerleaders — Peggy, Nick and Thomas O'Neill.

An unending note of appreciation to the following for believing in this obsessive photographer:

Tom Bevier, for his wonderful introduction and his support with ideas and expertise.

Roger Hicks, for listening to my book dreams and giving me support, advice and enthusiasm.

Michele Kapecky, a literary agent, a money lady, a marketing specialist, a friend and everything else that she had to be to get this book out.

Marcia Prouse, a friend and editor, for her special patience in editing the pictures and designing this book, and especially for the gentle persuasion she used to get me going in the right direction.

And a special thanks to Michelle Andonian, for enduring the last two years with my different moods, doubts and frustrations with this project. Thanks, Michelle, for showing me another side of myself through pictures and through your love.

Preface

I have always been drawn to people — especially the folksy, ebullient types with endless stories and simple wisdom, spinning yarn after yarn after yarn. You know — the "you don't mind if I bend your ears a bit?" type of people.

Their stories — with a mix of truth and fabrication — are sure to bring a chuckle.

Old Mission store owner Bob DeVol is one such person. I was so enchanted with his wit and stories that I almost forgot to take pictures.

The ends of his stories were always punctuated with a roar of laughter reaching from his belly.

Such is the feeling that I hope this book projects. That special richness of life that brings back warm memories and a smile. Nowhere is that richness more prevalent than in the numerous small towns and rural communities that dot Michigan.

The Main Street Michigan series, published in the Detroit Free Press — from which this book emerged — is a look at those small towns and the souls of the people in them.

Through photographs, I wanted to explore these ordinary people, looking for those little moments that reveal their ordinary but rich lives. I wanted them to show me what their lives entail — nothing fancy, nothing extraordinary — just them.

I remember a warm fall day driving in the heart of the Upper Peninsula. I saw a train slowly coming to a stop. I pulled over to take a picture.

The train stopped and out jumped the crew. It was lunchtime for this hefty bunch in the middle of what seemed like nowhere.

I followed the crew to an American Legion Post in nearby Little Lake. Between mounds of potatoes, roast beef and apple pie, the crew talked about life on the railroad in the 1940s and 1950s. I soaked it all in as the food on the table quickly disappeared.

Laurel, John, Joe and Philip had more than 176 years of experience on Michigan railroads. Some of the stories were sad, but the trainmen had a resilience about themselves. I photographed them as they ate, talked and laughed.

I followed them back to the train and took more pictures as they continued to talk and laugh. I jumped aboard and they showed me around.

The engine room exploded with noise as I felt the joy of my first train ride.

It was short-lived as I had to say goodby and jump from the train, which by now had picked up speed. Images of old Westerns flashed through my head as I landed in the loose gravel. I smiled as the train and its cargo of iron ore slowly disapppeared.

When the Main Street Michigan series started more than two years ago, the plan was simple — drive to small towns around the state and come up with photos and stories.

I drove from town to town anticipating what lay ahead, the stories to be told and the pictures to be taken.

A lot of the stories grew out of a visit to the local grocery store or gas station. While buying a snack or filling my gas tank, I would ask people about their towns. Who was doing what? Are there any special events coming up? Who is the town's character?

Other times, I would scour the pages of local newspapers for story ideas.

As the photostories appeared in the Free Press, I started to receive letters from people telling me about their towns.

In town after town, I found that what these communities lacked in size was made up for with caring people and hospitality.

They shared their lives with me, all the time wondering what made them noteworthy for this attention.

I was happy to find communities with a wonderful sense of values. These values bear a certain truth about humanity and our world, seen through the people, land and celebrations.

Imagine if you can a 70-year-old woman named Vi who welcomes people to her small diner. Vi always makes you feel good about yourself.

She sits on a bar stool next to you and starts a conversation. Before long, you are laughing and talking like you are long-lost friends.

Vi loves her diner and she wants her customers to enjoy it like she does.

I got a hug from Vi after my first visit to the diner. On my second visit, I got a hug and a kiss. By my third visit, I was just like family.

I stop by the Martin Diner whenever I am in the area. The food is good and the people are nice, but Vi makes it special. She has that feeling of intimacy — just like your grandmother or your favorite aunt.

Vi and the people at the Martin Diner are the epitome of what small-town Michigan is all about — friendly people, good home cooking and a warm atmosphere.

If there was a personal reason for my small-town chronicles it was because I wanted to meet the people who are the heart of small-town America.

When I was growing up on Guam, my schoolbooks were full of pictures and stories of the Midwest and small towns. Pictures of cornfields, snow scenes, farmers and main streets. The images in these schoolbooks were a new and magical world to me. All around on my tropical island were beaches and the ocean. There were two seasons, one rainy and the other dry.

The fascination resurfaced when I moved to Michigan after spending my college years in Missouri.

While I was on outstate assignments, I found myself leaving the freeways to explore Michigan's countryside. The fascination of my younger years now had tangible reality. As I drove through the small towns, I decided that I had to somehow use my new vocation to document this piece of Americana.

More than 60,000 miles later, I have found my personal piece of Americana — Michigan style. In more than two years, I have visited about 110 small towns and have taken more than 20,000 pictures. The best are here, but there are more favorite pictures that just couldn't be fitted into the book.

There are also a host of other towns that I just didn't have time to visit. And also numerous letters from people who wrote in with ideas. I appreciate the letters and wish I had more time to work on the ideas they contained.

One couldn't help but respect Frank Mattison. This 93-year-old fiddler was a folk hero to fellow musicians and to his neighbors in a host of surrounding towns. His modest charm and beautiful music inspired me.

Here was a truly gifted and talented man who was a symbol of longevity and love of music.

I spent several days in Smyrna with Frank, met his family, had dinner with him, listened to his story, traveled with him to his performances and enjoyed the music that sprang from his bow and violin.

My heart sank when his family called and said Frank had died. "You were an important part in my father's life," the message said.

After Frank died, I pored through the pictures I had taken over the last two years. This documentation of small-town life had taken an added twist. Now the pictures that were contemporary in nature were historical in perspective. Maybe it was always that way.

As a footnote, I feel a benevolence to this newly adopted state of mine.

My experiences are many and memorable.

My heart goes out to all my new friends and I hope the photographs and stories reflect them as they truly are.

— *Manny Crisostomo*

A parade-goer waits to catch a glimpse of the Vermontville Maple Syrup Parade.

Introduction

By THOMAS BeVIER

I know a man, handy with tools and shrewd at trading — qualities of his small-town mettle — who during the Depression gave, sight unseen, a Zenith radio for 15 acres of land on Manistee Lake near Kalkaska in northern lower Michigan.

Friends in his hometown, far to the south, thought him foolish because not only had he not seen the land, but there often were unpaid taxes owed in those hard times, and the property could only be reached with three days of bumpy driving over gravel and dirt roads.

He made the trip with his father. They stayed in a small log cabin, with a smoking stove, that had come with the trade. They walked the sandy land, which was covered with a spindly second growth of poplar and maple, and they visited with the people in the community by the shallow lake, a leftover settlement from the turn-of-the-century timber boom. In the evening, they watched the sun set over the lake.

"This is the most beautiful sunset I've ever seen," he told his father. "I think I'll hold on to this land."

When he returned home, his friends asked him about the land.

He didn't mention the sunset, even though that first impression explains why he owns the land to this day and returns each summer, making the trip in a single day by superhighway and paved county roads that have replaced the rough routes of his youth.

"I gave a pretty good radio for it," was all he said.

After all those years, perhaps as a sort of confirmation of the enduring attraction of such places, there is still a community on Manistee Lake.

During the course of my duties, which involve visiting small towns and out-of-the-way places in Michigan and writing about them, I happened there one evening in time for sunset. It may not have been the most beautiful sunset I'd ever seen, but it was of high rank, and it reinforced an attraction to the easeful rewards of places of slight population.

Afterward, I bought a cold drink at the store on the lake, one of the handful of businesses that cater to vacationers and to the several score of year-round residents.

"Pretty sunset," I said.

"Makes it all worthwhile," said the clerk in the store.

Sentiment, as embraced in the clerk's offhand comment, and fidelity to place, as shown by the old man's decades of commitment, figure in the essential purpose of this book. That purpose is to celebrate small-town and rural life in Michigan and to provide a subjective record of it on the state's sesquicentennial, 150 years after President Andrew Jackson signed the bill, on Jan. 26, 1837, making Michigan the 26th state.

For every town featured here, there are scores of others that could have served to illustrate small-town Michigan. The selections were arbitrary but never mean-spirited, and they usually are of a type, meant to represent groups of common heritage and purpose. If the reader gains a sense of the appeals and travails of small-town life, the purpose will have been served. Nothing done here, however, could replace the experience of a personal visit, of getting off the expressway and stopping in a single-stoplight place, to understand the good sense of the people who choose to live there.

Manny Crisostomo's pictures — his photographic impressions — carry the weight of this book's task. He documents moments of small-town life: people at work and at play, scenes of festivity and of serenity. By and large, these are not the sort of photographs you'd find on postcards, although a number of them would set new marks for that art form. Crisostomo has striven for the essence of what he characterizes as "Main Street Michigan." Usually, he has found it in the faces of the people.

Cumulatively, the portrait he presents is an optimistic one. That is not to say there are not problems: Some towns are barely getting by on nostalgia and wishful thinking; farming, still the lifeblood of many small towns, is a chancy vocation in these times of a national agricultural crisis; others lack economic diversity and so suffer or prosper with the fortunes of a single industry or business. And yet many have adapted: Nearly every village or burg claims an industrial park; retirees from the city, with certain incomes and remaining years of productivity, provide new energy; tourism, which draws harried city folks to the picturesque calm of many small towns, is a major growth industry in the state.

Through it all, small towns remain as places where people know and usually care about their neighbors, where there are fields or woods between the backyard and the horizon, and where sunsets get proper audience. The lights on Crisostomo's figurative Main Street are still bright.

There were 597 incorporated towns and cities in Michigan in 1980, according to the U.S. Census Bureau. They range from Detroit, with 1.2 million population, to places like Harrietta in Wexford County, with 139. Unincorporated communities, many of which have all the trappings, save for legal designation, of a town, are often even smaller. One of them, Eagle River — population about 35 — is the county seat of

Keweenaw County, near the tip of the peninsula of the same name that juts into Lake Superior at the western end of the Upper Peninsula.

About three-quarters of the state's 9.3 million population lives in towns or cities with more than 2,500 population. Not since 1920 has Michigan been considered a rural state. That was the year when the urban population first outnumbered the rural population, according to the Atlas of Michigan. In 1840, 96 percent of Michigan's population was rural.

The shift from rural to urban, of course, took its toll on small towns, even though much of the population growth in Michigan since 1920 has been with people from other states who came to work in the automobile plants and other industries. The state also drew population from foreign countries, notably to work in its copper and iron mines and to cut its rich stands of timber. Towns died in the process, but many of them were not built for longevity anyway, having been hastily thrown up to serve the lumber and mining booms.

The state's chief demographer, Laurence Rosen in the Department of Management and Budget, said the trend stopped in the 1970s and that some towns, particularly those in northern Michigan, where tourism development has been most aggressive, have had healthy gains. He projects an 8.4 percent increase, to 10 million, in the state's population by 2010, with 49 percent of the growth in the northern Lower Peninsula — roughly an area north of a line from Bay City to Muskegon.

Today, out of the 597 incorporated communities in the state, 184 have populations of less than 1,000; 148, between 1,000 and 2,500; 86, between 2,500 and 5,000, and 67 between 5,000 and 10,000.

A quandary for a book such as this is to decide when a town ceases to be small. Certainly, it is small if its population is under 2,500 and probably at around 5,000, but surely not when it goes over 10,000. At 10,000 and above a town should accept its fate and start thinking and acting like a city.

Almost all towns in Michigan, whatever their size, are on some sort of water. Lacking one of the

The Dansville Aggies marching band stops to perform in what residents called "one of the best parades in central Michigan."

14

Great Lakes at the doorstep, there are few that are far from a respectable-sized inland lake or don't have a meandering stream running through.

Even as water defines the state, it also defines its towns and cities. The near insularity of Michigan is unique among the states. The state's very name is an Indian word meaning "great water." Michigan's shoreline on Lake Erie, Lake Huron, Lake Michigan and Lake Superior measures 3,121 miles. There are 1,399 square miles of inland lakes and 36,350 miles of rivers and streams.

Early settlers, who followed the more transient fur trappers and French Jesuit explorers, settled near water. Indeed, the state's ready availability of water was a prime attraction. In return, the settlers brought with them the quality of permanence that had been previously lacking. That is the quality that has honed the state's character.

For instance, a group of Quakers from New York — the overwhelming majority of early settlers were from that state — followed the pattern in 1824 when they established a farming community on the Raisin River in southeastern Michigan, and called it Tecumseh. It was near the place where Chief Tecumseh, the Shawnee Indian leader, fought on the side of the British during the War of 1812.

The settlers used the river to power their gristmills. The community prospered even as it prospers today. The population is 7,320 and there is a firm economic base of industry and agriculture. Some residents, drawn by its turn-of-the-century charm, commute to work about 25 miles to Monroe or Ann Arbor or even farther to Toledo or Detroit. The homes, many of which bespeak the Greek Revival tastes of an earlier era, are well kept. Historic buildings downtown have been maintained and sometimes put to imaginative uses: The Chocolate Vault & Cake shop, for instance, was once a bank.

Tecumseh calls itself the Refrigerator Capital of the World because it is the home of Tecumseh Products, a compressor manufacturer that employs about 1,000 people. There are a dozen or so smaller industries, but in a five-minute drive

During the Upper Peninsula's long winters, Maxine Edwards tends to Germfask's snow-covered driveways and its 611 residents. Edwards is the township supervisor and also plows driveways.

from the center of town the landscape turns into rolling pasture and cropland. Many of the farms have been restored by gentleman farmers to a luster they never enjoyed with their original owners, reflecting an idealized modern-day version of farming, without calluses or cow manure.

The Quakers who established Tecumseh brought with them a steadfast will to succeed, to work as much as necessary and more. Their influence is not so apparent today, as in other towns where the influences of other churches also have faded.

A visit to Zeeland in southwestern Michigan, however, provides an idea of how important religion can be to a small town's character. In Zeeland, the rock-hard faith and adherence to the work ethic brought by Dutch settlers with their Reformed Church has been only slightly tempered since the town's founding in 1848.

Visitors to Zeeland who are used to a more relaxed approach to life's trials and tribulations in our laid-back society might find Zeeland overly staid and disciplined. But the town cannot be faulted for its orderliness, its pride and its prosperity.

Dowser Ben Thayer uses a forked stick to look for water in Fairview. Thayer has been "water witching" for about 50 years.

With a population of 4,764, there are 10 Reformed and Christian Reformed churches. (The latter group, which broke away from the original church in 1857, is generally considered the more liberal of the two.) Sunday is strictly for worship in Zeeland. All stores are closed. If you happen to run out of gas, the police will see that you get some, but there are no gas stations open. Residents do not mow their lawns on Sunday, either.

There is practically no crime or unemployment. There are 6,000 jobs in the town of 5,000 people. Many families have lived in Zeeland for several generations, which gives the community a sense of continuity. The largest employer, with 1,800 workers, is Herman Miller Inc., an international leader in the design and manufacture of office furnishings. The streets are paved, taxes are low and the municipal coffers are full.

Mayor Donald Disselkoen, who is a Republican of Dutch ancestry — credentials helpful to any Zeeland politician — summed it up this way: "This is a sincere, God-fearing community."

In the 19th Century, across the southern part of the Lower Peninsula, agriculture was the primary reason for development. In the upper two-thirds of the Lower Peninsula and the eastern third of the Upper Peninsula it was mainly lumbering.

When the tree cutting began with a fury around 1840, the white and red pine were viewed as "inexhaustible." In retrospect, Michigan's Pulitzer Prize-winning historian, Bruce Catton, referred to "inexhaustible" as "that fatal Michigan word." It had been used first to apply to fur and later for lumber and mines.

Lumbering changed the very face of the state. Vast stands of pine were cut. By 1897, 160 billion board feet had been taken, an amount that, according to one estimate, was enough to floor the entire state of Michigan and leave enough to do Rhode Island.

During the lumber era, some towns were established overnight and abandoned almost as quickly as the trees were gone. In others, the people who settled the towns stayed on, getting by any way they could. Scores of towns died, without much ceremony, but many held on against all odds.

One that is still holding on is Comins, a settlement of about 125 people. You have to strain to find it on the map in Oscoda County, 15 miles north of Mio on M-33.

Comins was at the end of the line of a logging railroad built shortly after the 1873 arrival of the first settler, a logger from Bangor, Maine, named Coolidge Comins. The railroad was abandoned in 1927 and some of the old-timers can still remember the last train out.

Comins depends mainly on deer hunters and occasional tourists. Its main attraction is its past. It is uncomfortable to speculate about its future. There are two — not one, but two — museums, a restaurant, a gas station and a post office. An old hotel has been converted to a gift shop and ice cream parlor.

Until recently, there wasn't much to remind visitors of Comins' end-of-the-line status. That deficiency, however, was corrected when local movers and shakers managed to cajole various politicians and the Michigan National Guard into trucking in a 26-ton caboose. It rests on 40 feet of track beside the still-standing depot of the old Au Sable & Northwestern Railroad.

Cedar, a town of similar size that also was a product of the lumber era, is faring better over near the shore of Lake Michigan in Leelanau County. Polish immigrants settled there before the turn of the century and have held on, thanks to summer tourists and the town's allegiance to Holy Rosary Catholic Church.

Other towns in the county, which also have an ethnic heritage (Maple City, German; Lake Leelanau, French; Suttons Bay, Norwegian), also are sharing in the booming development of tourism in northwestern Michigan.

Few towns can beat Cedar for picturesque appeal. As you crest a high hill, it nestles below in a narrow valley. Fresh Polish sausage can be purchased at its groceries and in July thousands of downstaters party in the streets during Polefest. Things are going so well in Cedar that the town has decided to incorporate.

Some former lumbering towns have been able to make their own breaks.

In 1967, Rose City — founded in 1892 — had a population of around 500 and was rapidly losing that. The town's bank had failed in the Depression and there was little industry. The streets weren't paved, the sewer system was substandard and what businesses remained were generally marginal operations.

Bernard Card, a hard-talking booster and seller of metal buildings, called a meeting in 1967, and the Rose City Businessmen's Association was founded. One of the first things the association did was send more than 200 letters to manufacturers, trying to attract them to the Ogemaw County town 20 miles north of West Branch and Interstate-75. The town got one taker. A nail manufacturer came to talk it over. He said he liked the location because the town is near I-75. He said there was plenty of labor available. He said everything was just perfect except that the town didn't have a bank and without a bank he wasn't interested.

Card and the others got a bank, a branch of the Farmers & Merchants State Bank of Hale. Then they tried again.

Rose City's population has grown to 661. There are 13 light manufacturing plants, whose

Laura Yenz gets her pony, Snowflake, ready for the youngster's first ride in the Dansville Memorial Day parade.

products range from seat belt parts to plastic toys. Among Rose City's distinctions is the claim of having the nation's "largest battery of computer-controlled automatic screw machines" in its Header Products plant.

Card claims it's the best place in the world to live, which provides an indication of the conviction brought to promoting his town.

In the hearts and minds of most Americans, the typical small town owes its existence to farming. There should be cornfields and wheat fields on the other side of the town limits, with the town's fortune depending on the weather and the unfathomable eccentricities of the Chicago Board of Trade.

If that's what they're after, they should go to Bad Axe. Bad Axe, quaintly named and proud of it, is the county seat of Huron County in the Thumb. It is the richest agricultural county in Michigan.

Bad Axe got its name because an early surveyor, Rudolph Papst, found a worn ax embedded in a white pine in 1861. It was "an awfully bad ax," he said. Bad Axe was incorporated as a village in 1885.

During the winter and early spring, the flat land around Bad Axe stretches to the horizon, broken by only an occasional stand of trees and farmsteads. It is a lonely, windswept scene. But then the winter wheat pokes through and soon after, when the ground is firm and dry enough to support tractors, the planting of corn, beans and sugar beets begins. You'd never guess that Bad Axe was involved in a fire that blazed over much of the Thumb in 1881. By summer, it is a picture of fertility, and conversation on the downtown streets buzzes with anticipation over the coming harvest.

The town itself has maintained its purpose, serving farmers and their families. Sturdy work clothes can be purchased in Bad Axe and the chicken fried steak is super. You come away thinking that as long as people have to eat there will be a place in this world for Bad Axe.

To leave the Lower Peninsula and cross the 8,614-foot-long bridge, more than 500 feet above the waters of the Straits of Mackinac, is to enter a region where almost all towns are small. Even the largest UP town, Marquette, has a population of only 21,666.

At the approach to the bridge, is Fort Michilimackinac, restored to the way archeologists say it looked when the French built it in 1715. And off to the right, as you mount the bridge, is Mackinac Island, the state's most successful tourist attraction. No motorized vehicles are allowed on the island — the horse reigns there — to detract from the Victorian appeal of the place. And Mackinac Island also has a fort, one the French built between 1779 and 1781, to replace Michilimackinac. Later, the British occupied Fort Mackinac, and then the Americans. It has been owned by the State of Michigan since 1895.

The forts are in keeping with the colonizing spirit that settled the UP, one of the most isolated and thinly populated (only 330,000 people in 16,446 square miles) areas in the United States. The winters are long and hard.

Since the 17th Century, the people who have gone to the UP usually have wanted to take something out. The fur trappers were the first, followed by the copper and iron miners and the lumberjacks. To live in the UP is to develop an independent way of thinking and to have certain reservations about outsiders.

The carnival rides are a big attraction during the weekend-long Maple Syrup Festival in Vermontville.

The people of the UP are found in small towns. They know their neighbors' kith and kin, each other's good points and bad, and they help each other out when the going gets tough.

Many of the towns were built by mining or lumber barons. One of the more ambitious of those ventures was Gwinn, founded in 1908 at the instigation of the corporate predecessor of the present Cleveland Cliffs Iron Co. to take advantage of the Swanzy Iron Range.

Mining, both copper and iron, is a dying occupation in the UP, and if towns that owe their existence to mining are to survive they must find other economic reasons for being. Gwinn, in Marquette County, found the U.S. Air Force. It is the home of K.I. Sawyer Air Force Base, which employs more than 5,000 military and civilian personnel and has an annual payroll of more than $92 million.

Gwinn is a place worth keeping. The downtown is set on a square with a park in the middle crowded with tall pines. There is a bandstand in the park, and the Escanaba River, rich with trout, flows beside it. On first impression, Gwinn is like a bit of New England.

The original plans for the town were drawn by Abram Garfield, the architect son of President James Garfield. The plan included a community center with an indoor swimming pool and a gymnasium. As an indication of the ethnic variety found in the UP — many European immigrants were brought in to work the mines and fell the trees — the center's dedication ceremonies were repeated in eight languages.

The UP has had a boom-and-bust economy from the beginning. Nowhere is that more obvious than at Calumet on the Keweenaw Peninsula. Right now, it's bust. When you get to Calumet, you're about as far away in the state as you can get. It's 500 miles from the state capital in Lansing and 585 miles from Detroit, the largest city.

Calumet, in Houghton County, which once supported a population of about 50,000, and has the empty buildings to prove it, now has only about 1,000 residents. It's hanging on to its identity as a small town that once had city aspirations.

East Coast investors built Calumet in the mid-1800s around the rich copper mines. It attracted nearly every nationality you can think of and a few besides: English, Finns, French Canadians, Slovenians, Croatians, Italians, Germans, Poles, Swedes, Norwegians, Hungarians, Irish, Romanians. But the boom ended. The last mine in the immediate area closed in 1968 after a bitter strike. (The only remaining copper mine in the UP is at White Pine, in Ontonagon County southwest of Calumet.)

The Eastern Europeans built their Catholic churches, the Scandinavians their Lutheran

An antique car heading home from a parade passes the West Benton United Methodist Church, just outside Potterville.

ones. The steeples of the churches, all but a few of which have been abandoned, are sad reminders of what Calumet used to be. The opera house, where Lillian Russell, John Philip Sousa and Sarah Bernhardt once played, has been restored as an historic landmark, but it is underutilized.

Still, Calumet is a good place to offer a toast to small towns, particularly if you do it at Shute's 1890 Bar.

The proprietor, Bernie Shute, whose father owned the bar before him, can vividly recall how things used to be and he has more than a few cantankerous ideas about how they might be.

"All it takes is this," he says, rubbing his thumb and forefinger together to indicate money.

But that's not all it takes, and nobody knows that better than Shute. It takes people like him, who are willing to work more than 100 hours a week to keep a business going and who, when he walks around town, entertains a feast of memories and a groaning board of hopes.

"Calumet is a pretty good place, even now," he says, drawing a beer.

So here's to Calumet, and to all small towns in Michigan. The past is found in them, as well as the promise and uncertainties of the future.

People of character

"I have been here for 57 years and have found the greatest people on Earth. And that's the truth." — Mary Jane Pardee of Garden

Beyond the postcards and travel posters of Michigan lies a land of small towns with people of extraordinary character and a compassionate view of life.

The back roads of the Great Lakes State are bent and narrow trails that lead to Hope and Bliss and Negaunee, little-known small towns whose valued tradition and moral fiber dominate them.

These are small towns where the main street is the heart but the people are the soul.

As a lot, the residents are ordinary people but full of unique nuances and appeal, full of life and stories and simple moments. And their values — hard work, sincerity and love of land — are the essential components of Michigan's true character.

Dansville

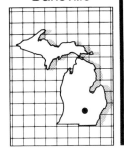

The Dansville Aggies marching band stops at the center of town to perform. There were about four times as many parade-goers as the entire population of 480. The parade was part of a celebration that included bingo, a barn dance, a chicken barbecue and hot-air balloon rides.

Galesburg

Glenn Bell looks out to the town of Galesburg from the bakery he and his wife, Phyllis, have operated since May 2, 1936. The couple celebrated a half-century of baking in the southwestern Michigan town of 1,400 with free coffee and doughnuts. They received a special tribute from the Michigan Legislature and governor.

Calumet

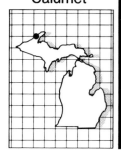

A 1956 Plymouth Belvedere sits frozen in time in front of Calumet's 88-year-old former firehouse, now vacant.

Mackinac Island

Nick Caidotte, 57, waits for the afternoon ferry from Mackinac Island to St. Ignace. A longtime island resident, Caidotte works there during the summer and relaxes in St. Ignace during the winter.

Mackinac Island 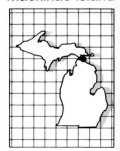 Horses are led to the ferry to be taken off the island and delivered to a farm in the Upper Peninsula.

Negaunee 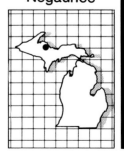 Many of the downtown buildings along Iron Street in Negaunee were built at the turn of the century when the mining industry was booming.

Germfask

Germfask volunteer fire fighters pose in front of the fire station in the town of 611 people. From left: Arthur Leffler, Jim Tuttle, Barbara Ackley, Jim Burton, Barbara Leffler, Jerry Jack and Robert Campbell. The town has had a volunteer fire department since 1952.

Old Mission

Bob DeVol remembers climbing a steam radiator to get to the candy at Lardie's Grocery Store in Old Mission. He was about 10 then. Fifty-one years later, DeVol can have all the candy he wants at Lardie's. He's been the owner for the last 23 years.

At the Martin Diner in Martin, owner Violet McCarren serves home-cooked meals with a smile.

Vi, as she is better known, admits to a love affair with the people who come to this former Kalamazoo streetcar, now located in this town of 600.

"This is a lovable place," says Vi, 70. "That's why they come here, so they can be themselves."

The diner has been under Vi's ownership for 30 years.

Vi helps with nearly every job in the diner, and when the place gets crowded, she takes orders, cooks or washes the dishes. But most of the time she has her hands around a coffee cup and is chatting and laughing with the customers.

Martin

Martin Diner owner Vi McCarren laughs and jokes with her customers, above, in her diner, housed in a former Kalamazoo streetcar. "We are crazy but a fun bunch here," she says. At far left, traffic passes by during the early morning hours.

31

Waitress Sandra Holden chats with the regulars, at left. The yellow diner is a favorite among area farmers and factory workers and a novelty for tourists. Above, life at the diner is reflected on the cigaret machine during the morning hours.

Bay Mills

DeVerna Hubbard remembers going as a child to the Point Iroquois lighthouse with her family. "When I was a kid, I thought it would be neat to live in a lighthouse," she says. She has her wish 50 years later: Hubbard is caretaker of the lighthouse in the Hiawatha National Forest.

Eagle River

Twenty-two of the 35 year-round residents of Eagle River gather for a group portrait in front of the Keweenaw County Courthouse, at far right.

Marion

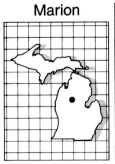

Ben Fergeson, 45, drives his lawnmower near Marion's main intersection, at left. Fergeson mows about 50 lawns during the summer months. "I loaf around in the winter," he says. Above, retirees Stanley Roper, behind the tree, and Leland Watkins lounge with Watkins' dog, Brownie. The 1,500 residents support themselves mostly with farming, and work in nearby gas fields and several small factories.

Five Mile Creek  Leroy and Anna Stanton walk their dog, Tiny, during the early evening hours in Five Mile Creek, a small settlement just north of Harbor Springs. The couple converted an old sawmill and made it their retirement home.

Mio  Some kids teased, others frolicked and a few stood patiently while waiting in line for ice cream during a warm summer afternoon in Mio, the county seat of Oscoda County.

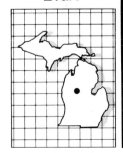

Evart

Evart Police Capt. Don Schmidt watches his granddaughter Shasta Hunter, in front of City Hall in downtown Evart.

Harbor Springs

A youngster samples some of the wares outside a store in downtown Harbor Springs.

Strongs

Blacksmith Russell Johnson, right, and Floyd Morningstar share some conversation and similar gestures outside his business in Strongs. Johnson has been a blacksmith for more than 50 years.

Hulbert

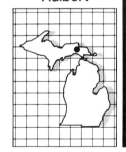

Jo Harrison makes eye contact with a customer in her Macjo gift shop, gas station and motel. Harrison keeps the highway business open seven days a week, with the help of a weekend assistant. "It is better to wear out than rust out, my mother used to say."

Garden Corners

Liz and George Streeter sit with their dog Sissy in front of a Hawaiian mural at the Leilani Motel in Garden Corners, at left.

National Mine

A snow-covered face is an occupational hazard for a UP pooch, above, but it doesn't seem to faze this curly-coated mongrel in National Mine. The pooch keeps a lonely vigil for the mail carrier.

Centreville

On the next pages, an Amish boy heads for his Centreville home with his dog tagging along after a day of working in the fields with his father. St. Joseph County is thought to have the largest Amish population in the state.

Galien

Albert Payne, at far left, is a full-time farmer with a full-time hobby. The Galien farmer works his corn, soybeans, wheat, oats and hay, and tends 120 cattle. For the last 35 years, Payne also has put together what he calls one of the biggest collections of antique horse-drawn equipment outside of museums.

Smyrna

The fiddling family from Smyrna: the late Frank Mattison with his daughter, Francis Geiger, and granddaughter, Karlene Johnson. Grandson Justin Johnson is in front. They are playing on a bridge near their homes.

Omer

Loyal Leinaar and his wife, Marie, return their lawn chairs after sitting out most of the afternoon in Omer. Loyal, at 83, is Omer's oldest resident. "It's a quiet town," says Loyal. "It's a nice place to live.

Hope

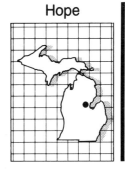

John and Lafey Leuenberger, 90 and 82 respectively, look over pictures of their children and grandchildren after 64 years of marriage. John retired from farming and Lafey retired from teaching in Hope area one-room schools.

Charlotte

Dog lover Pearl Keeley, far left, kisses Dinkey as she holds Baby, two of the dogs at her trailer home outside Charlotte. At left, pictures of Keeley's late husband, Stan, join a portrait of Little Bit, her first dog. Below, Keeley lectures Wire as some of her other dogs gather around the couch.

Pearl Keeley is a dog lover. The 72-year-old widow, who is retired, shares her trailer home outside Charlotte with 25 dogs. That's nothing compared with the 100 or so dogs she used to keep at her Lansing dry cleaning business.

"I just can't take a dog to an animal pen," says Keeley. "A dog doesn't have a chance there."

Keeley's life revolves around Wee Wee, Missy, Princess, Goldy, Dinky, Wire, Hutty, Carrot Top, Buster, Baby and Champ, to name just a few.

"Everyone has a name. And every one of these dogs just loves me to death."

Garden

Mary Jane Pardee, affectionately called "Grandma Pardee" or "Aunt Mary," has a warm relationship with residents of Garden, a town of 296 people. "I have been here for 57 years and have found the greatest people on Earth," says Pardee.

Mass City

Barber Frank Saaranen is reflected alone in his shop in Mass City. Little has changed in 37 years at Frank's Barber Shop — not the little old building, not the porcelain and leather barber chair and not the sparse furnishings.

near Engadine

A truck speeds by on M-20 as the railroad heads out into the sunset in the Upper Peninsula, at left.

Sears

A stop sign is all that remains of this road, above, overgrown with grass, just south of the village of Sears.

Hulbert

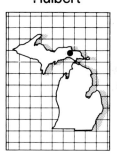

On the next pages, wild turkeys trot down Hulbert's main street.

The hard-work ethic

"Work is my pastime. Retiring is for lazy people" — 77-year-old farmer Avery Babcock of Roscommon

There is a certain pride among workers in small towns. Many are more concerned about making good lives for themselves and their families than in their paychecks at the end of a workweek. To be sure, they take pride in working hard, but they don't get caught up in the daily rat race common to urban living.

Work and life are intertwined for:

• A master blacksmith, who says, "I just make a living and I never got rich." He was happy to make $20 a day.

• A story-telling storekeeper, who says, "We'll never be rich or famous, but we make a comfortable living."

• An 80-year-old gas station owner, who says, "It is better to wear out than rust out."

• A second-generation barber, who says, "If you are going to make it in rural America, you have to be more dedicated to your work."

• A teenager, who will be among the next generation of farmers, and who says, "I think when the times are tough, that's a test of what you are."

Germfask

During the Upper Peninsula's long winters, Maxine Edwards tends to Germfask's snow-covered driveways and its 611 residents. Edwards is the township supervisor and also plows driveways. "I used to do 50 driveways two years ago," says Edwards. "I can't do it now with all the rest of the stuff, like township stuff and 'tending meetings."

David Charles, who has been with the mine for 25 years, stands in the maintenance room below ground.

White Pine

The Jeep ride down the incline, which miners call a drift, was five miles long. At the bottom, the drift was 2,100 feet below the surface.

"This is a very pleasant working environment," says Russell Wood, president of Copper Range Co., which was formed by employes and managers who reopened the state's last copper mine in White Pine in 1985.

Wood, who has spent all his working life in mines in the United States and South

The mine's drifts angle for five miles to a depth of 2,100 feet. Below, the miners' changing room stands empty waiting for the mine to re-open in 1985.

America, says the mine, its mill and refinery are a state-of-the-art operation, and that replacing them would cost more than $600 million.

When ore is mined, there are only about 20 pounds of copper per ton. But the result, after the ore goes through crushers, separators, smelters and other refining processes, is copper that is 99.99 percent pure.

"You won't find a more efficient operation anywhere," Wood says.

Strongs

Russell Johnson works in his blacksmith shop behind his son's grocery store and gas station in Strongs. The tiny shop is full of tools he has collected over the years. Here, he holds a hammer he made 30 years ago.

Newberry

Lumberjack Tuffy Burton sits amid cut lumber outside Newberry. Four years earlier, Burton was drawing unemployment checks; now he is cashing in on the lumber boom.

Mackinac Island

Eight days before Christmas, while nearly everyone else rushes to get shopping done, the ferry to Mackinac Island rushes food and supplies before the lake freezes over.

Operating out of St. Ignace, the ferry Mackinac Islander runs as often as four times a day, six days a week. There are extra runs for supplies on the only operating ferry from the Arnold Transit Co. that time of year. The ferry shuts down Jan. 2, or earlier if ice gets too heavy in the Straits of Mackinac. It reopens in April.

"We are transporting everything and anything to get people through the winter," says Senior Capt. Paul Allers.

The list includes food, oil, gas, construction supplies for the islands' hotels — and a winter's supply of beer.

It takes about 30 minutes for the round-trip. "We are loaded every trip," Allers says.

But the ferry is at the mercy of the weather.

"It varies from year to year," Allers says. "We go on all kinds of weather until the ice gets heavy."

Deckhand Roger Horn, far left above, gets ready for docking on Mackinac Island. The Mackinac Islander made a special trip to deliver gasoline. Above, the crew unloads gas on one of two docks on the island. Left, the crew, left to right: Bill Squires, Ray Wilkins, Roger Horn, Paul Allers, Dick Graham and Ron Halberg.

Yalmer

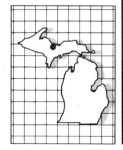

Sue Welch stands in front of Welch General Store in Yalmer. Welch, 37, is a "100 percent Swede" and owner of the store in the town of 300 people. The storefront is the original from the late 1800s.

Three Oaks

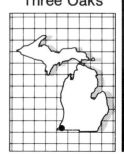

Ed Drier serves as butcher and unofficial museum curator at the Drier Butcher Shop. The shop, a national historic site that has been a butcher shop since shortly after the Civil War, is filled with tools, fixtures and antiques from the 19th Century.

Allen

It has been more than 20 years since a younger Colonel William Pengelly frequented a flea market booth owned by Eva Panzich. The couple married and opened their own antique shop in Allen.

Romeo

The Valentine spirit is hale and hearty in Romeo — as it should be in a place with such a name — thanks in great part to Sherm and Linda Rundles. For Valentine's Day, they turn out more than 100 varieties of candies from more than 1,000 pounds of chocolate.

Hulbert

Jo Harrison, owner of the Macjo gift shop, gas station and motel in Hulbert, chats with Eugene Stogene, of Montreal, as he fills up his tow truck during one of her many late nights of work. Harrison left a nursing job and bought the property for the highway business with her late husband in 1945.

Hulbert Paradise

Melinda Cree discusses the Lord's Prayer during the children's part of services, far left, at the Paradise United Methodist Church. The Iowa native does double duty as intern minister in churches in Paradise and Hulbert.

New Buffalo

Paul Baxter, a crossing guard for 25 years, holds a tired Jamie Pierce as they wait for the traffic light to change at a New Buffalo intersection. New Buffalo High School dedicated its 1986 yearbook to him. "I have seen them all grow up," Baxter says.

Barber Ron Heckman reads the paper as he waits for customers after opening his barbershop at 6:30 a.m. in downtown Pigeon.

Pigeon

A lot of stories and gossip have been passed along at the Heckman Barber Shop in Pigeon over the last 44 years.

"A lot come here for haircuts and gossip," says Ron Heckman. "Then they go out and tell people and I get into trouble."

Heckman has kept busy running the barbershop since his father died. He is ready to give haircuts at 6:30 a.m. and puts in 11 hours a day Tuesday through Saturday. "If you are going to make it in rural America, you have to be more dedicated to your work."

A lot of older customers come to the shop to "chew the fat" with Heckman and whomever else is there. A lot of those old-timers also were there when his father was the barber.

If gossip is slow, they usually talk about the good old days. "Saturday nights in Pigeon used to be fun," says Floyd Collison. "They didn't have television then. People used to visit each other a lot more back then."

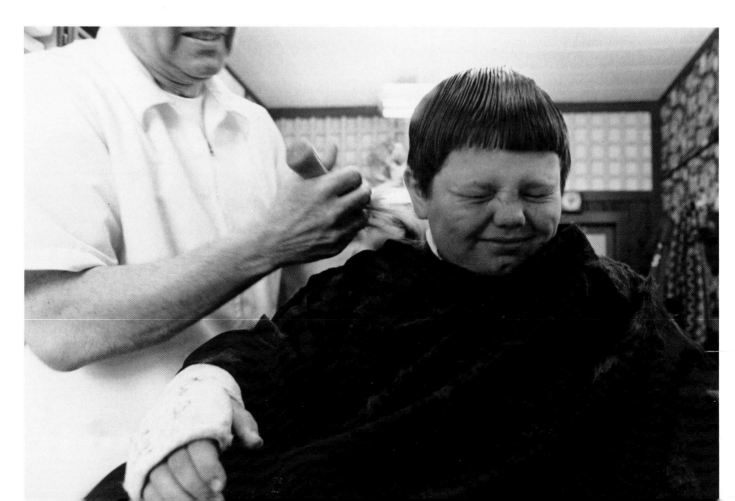

Heckman cuts Dick Buchholz's hair under the heads of deer, bear and moose shot by Heckman's father. Below left, Tom Blome grimaces as he gets his haircut. Tom and his brother, Bob, go to the barbershop every two weeks.

Route 36 quietly winds through the farms that dot the tightly knit farming community of Dansville. The farmers are out planting early, taking advantage of the warm weather and hoping for a good year.

Also hoping that the farmers have a good year is Dansville veterinarian George Harris. The robust vet spends most of his time working on farm animals. Economic uncertainty in the farming industry has affected Harris and some of his farm clients, the same clients he has had for 28 years.

Harris works Monday through Saturday, about 8 a.m. to 5:30 p.m., and is on call 24 hours a day.

"When I retire, I'll still do some veterinary work," he says. "Right here till I die."

Dansville

George Harris treats a cow after it gave birth, far left. Harris talks with farmer Larry Nelson, above, about how to keep his herd healthy. Left, a lunch break gives Harris time to change his shirt. He goes through three a day.

79

It's a lonely job being an oil field pumper. For the last 15 years, Walt Heminger has been working alone tending wells and storage tanks south of Morley.

Every morning, Heminger gets into a truck and drives through woods and farmland to the 13 pumping wells and four disposal wells in the Reynolds Oil Field.

He oils and checks the pumps and the engines that run them, gauges the level of oil in the storage tanks and does general maintenance.

Heminger was born and raised in Morley. "It is right handy that I don't have to drive to work.

"I kind of enjoy being alone and I like the woods," he says. "I enjoy watching the deer."

Morley

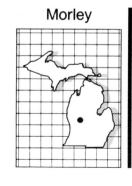

Walt Heminger, above left, stands in a tin shack for the engine that runs the oil pump. Top, Heminger puts some muscle into the flywheel to start the engine that runs the oil pump. Above, Heminger tends to the oil wells. He heads out to tend to the oil pumps, left.

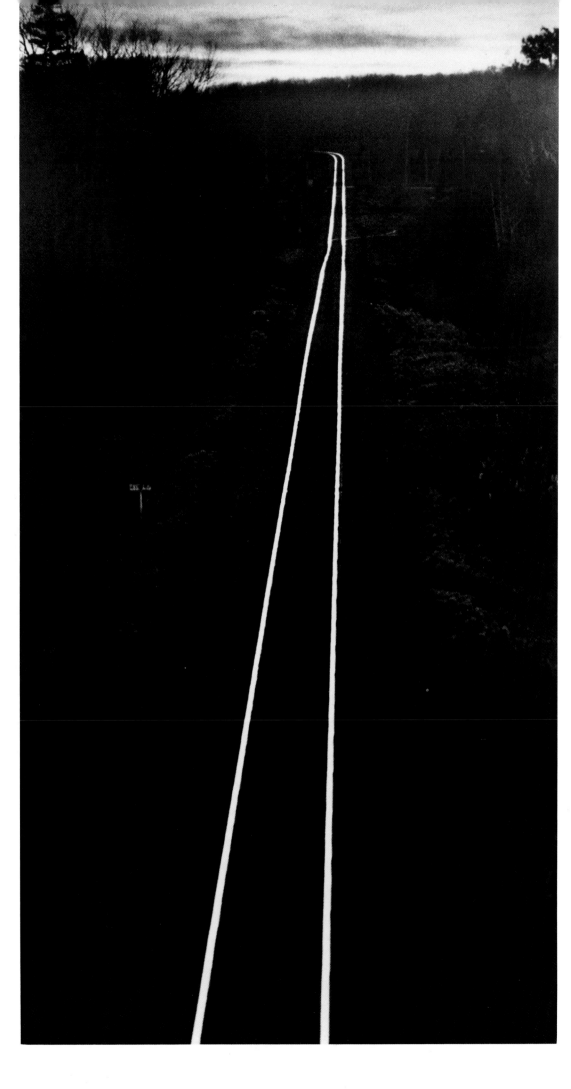

Little Lake

More than 176 years of work on the railroads rides with this crew in the Upper Peninsula. From left, Philip Dubord, brakeman; John MacGiles, brakeman; Laurel Olson, engineer, and Joe Miller, conductor. During the boom days in the 1940s, the railroads were busy carrying iron ore and copper from the UP mines. This crew hauls iron on a 12-hour, 122-mile round-trip from Empire Mine in Palmer to Escanaba.

A love of the land

"I was borned and raised here. And I never left." — *Blacksmith Russell Johnson of Strongs*

This is a state of Great Lakes, undisturbed forests, arching sand dunes and rich, fertile soil. It also is a state where people have a deep appreciation for this wealth of natural treasures.

Nowhere is this love more evident than in the people of rural and small-town Michigan.

There is beauty everywhere — from the edges of the Great Lakes, to the carved remnants of copper country in the Upper Peninsula, to the farmland that extends from the Thumb throughout the Lower Peninsula in this hand-shaped state.

But love of the land is less geographic than it is a personal and communal affection.

It is evident in a farmer's tender caring for the acres of land that have provided his family's livelihood for generations.

It shows in the travels of people who spend summers along Michigan's spectacular coasts.

It is evident in the community spirit among UPers as they tackle long winters with diving temperatures and 300 inches of snow.

It can be heard in the buzzing of chain saws by lumberjacks as they break the quiet in the forest.

Fairview

Dowser Ben Thayer uses a forked stick to look for water in Fairview. Thayer has been "water witching" for about 50 years. "Well, I guess you can call it a gift," says Thayer. He is called in to make sure there is water on the property before the owner digs a well. He usually gets $10 for his efforts, and says he is about 90 percent accurate.

Roscommon

Looking over his 200-acre farm near Roscommon, 77-year-old Avery Babcock shows no signs of slowing down. He had just shipped 120 bales of hay and one of his barns was full of grain from a harvest.

"Work is my pastime," he says. "Retiring is for lazy people."

Babcock lives with his wife, Louella, on the Au Sable Township farm he has had since 1942. His 14 children have all moved and have families of their own.

"I have always wanted to be a farmer, ever since my earliest recollections," Babcock says. "Even if there is no money in it, I still love it."

Farmer Avery Babcock, above left, heads to his garden to dig potatoes. He also grows green beans, tomatoes, strawberries and raspberries. Above, he wipes his face during a hot spell. Left, he checks the soil for mowing hay. He has had the tractor for 30 years.

Babcock opens his barn, left, where he stores his hay. Above, he plays his harmonica for his wife, Louella. "I can't read a note of music, but I have been playing better than 60 years," he says.

Mennonite farmers Glenn and Erma Maust, with their lamb, Patches, stand in front of their 80-year-old barn in Bay Port. While doing her afternoon chores, right, Erma is followed closely by Patches. Below right, Glenn shovels corn to some of the 1,200 hogs.

Bay Port farmers Glenn and Erma Maust can still remember the hogs they received as a wedding gift.

"We started with gilt pigs (225-pound sows) as a gift from Dad," Erma says. "They multiplied and we sold them to market. That's how we made our farm payments."

The hardworking Mennonite couple turned those few gilts and 40 rented acres into a farm that now includes more than 1,200 hogs, 200 cattle and 370 acres.

"We started from scratch and worked and saved," says Erma.

Their grandparents came to Michigan to farm. The tradition continues into the fourth generation with the couple's eight children.

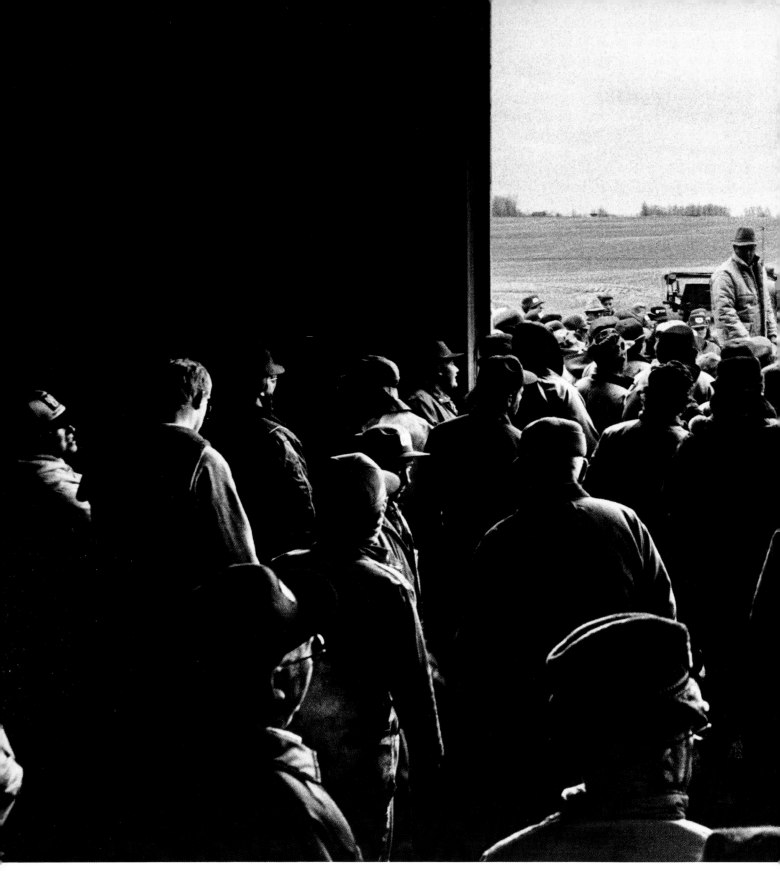

Carsonville

Carsonville farmers listen to the auctioneer as he sells off farm equipment and memorabilia from Leon Smith's 40 years of farming. After the last of his equipment was gone, Smith said, "It's like giving your daughter away at the wedding. You're sad, but happy."

It was a small-town auction that had just about everything. The items for bid included toys, tools, quilts, candy, salami, cookies, Easter baskets, toilet-bowl cleaners, ammonia, tea sets and something called imaging powder that was sold for 25 cents even though the new owners couldn't figure out what it was for.

About 25 people attended the weekend auction in a one-room building in White Cloud.

Some were shop owners looking for merchandise, but most were simply looking for things for their homes or shopping for toys for their children and grandchildren.

"We buy at wholesale and sell to the people whatever they say it's worth," says auction owner Ken Young. "Usually, they get deals at half the retail cost."

Earl Buttleman waits to pay for the items he bought, above left. Josh Glen Ringler, below left, shows off a toy gun his father bought for him. Behind him are, from left, Richard Buttleman, Keith Bullis, Charles Bullis and Earl Buttleman. Two women chat, above, during the bidding. Below, Doris Mock leaves with her purchases, including a box of cereal priced lower, she says, than at her grocery store.

White Cloud

95

Amish boys sit in a wagon in front of an 1812 original Conestoga wagon that Albert and Ellen Payne drove 1,000 miles to Valley Forge, Pa., on the Bicentennial wagon train in 1976.

Auction-goers help unload a Chicago stock wagon just purchased by Janet and Stanley Masiwchuk.

Farmer and carriage collector Albert Payne walked into his empty barn and felt a twinge of sadness. After nearly four decades of collecting antique horse-drawn equipment, the barns and sheds that once were filled to the rafters were barren. Payne held a public auction and sold 720 lots that included 69 antique carriages, horses and

96

Irva Fry and Dave Rodrick carry a life-size mechanical horse into the tent to be auctioned.

oxen, farm machinery, toys, antiques and miniature and heavy wagons.

"I miss all of them," says the 68-year-old farmer from Galien. "I'll go down to my barn and see those empty hooks. It looks pretty barren."

The public auction held on his 200-acre farm drew more than 3,000 farmers, nostalgia buffs, Amish and Mennonite farmers and collectors from more than 12 states.

The biggest sale was a restored road coach made by Walters Co. of London — sold for $25,000 to a California couple. The same couple bought a 1906 Gypsy wagon, shipped from England in 1906, for $12,500.

By the end of the day everything was sold except for an original 1812 Conestoga wagon. "I'm glad the Conestoga didn't sell," says Payne. "I'll never find another one like that."

Payne has yet to recover from selling his "hobby."

"I don't think I'll ever recover," he says. "Just like an old tire that gets flat. You need a lot more patches to keep the air in."

Galien

Some of the items for sale sit on display, above. Far left, Amish boys look at an ornate Gypsy wagon. Middle left, a buyer shows his bid number to the auctioneer after purchasing a piece. Left, this Conestoga wagon didn't sell.

Faces in the crowd

Top left on opposite page, Don Williams, with whip in hand, drives one of the wagons around the auction; bottom left, Bengamin Martin, a Mennonite, stands in front of a reproduction of a pony-size Victoria carriage, and the crowd watches the bidding. Above left on this page, Floyd Miller takes a seat on an 1870 thrashing machine; below left, Cecil Swank and Ernest Shaw rest, and above, Craig Askins has a good perch atop a log cart.

Tipton

Gary Abner holds a kid in front of his 250 goats in his Tipton barn. Abner and his wife, Nancy, have the first and largest licensed goat dairy in Michigan.

Remus

An abandoned house provides shade during the summer for some Angora goats in Remus. The goats' coats are sheared for mohair.

Whitefish Pt.

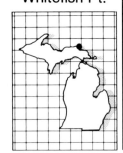

The Whitefish Point Lighthouse stands sentinel on the sandy shore of Lake Superior.

Northport

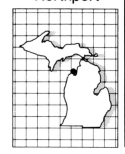

The Old Mission Lighthouse stands against a cloudy winter sky.

Centerville Twp.

Snowdrifts cover the front door of the Centerville Township Hall in Leelanau County.

Pentwater

Drifting sand dunes cover fences on the shore of Lake Michigan near Pentwater, right.

Victoria

On the next pages, old log houses are about all that remains from the mining boom.

Carson City

Summer laundry blows in the breeze in this yard east of Carson City.

Harbor Beach

Coast Guard
Second Lt. Robert
Michalski walks the
long boardwalk to
the Coast Guard
station in Harbor
Beach, left.

Pigeon

Silos from the
Pigeon Cooperative
loom over this
Thumb farming
community.

Afton

The cost of gas — 42 cents a gallon — on a pump reflects a time gone by in Afton.

The joys of youth

"I have been coming here every year since I was eight years old. I loved the beautiful gowns and the astonishment of the girls that won." — Christine Rigozzi, Miss Bangor 1986, about the beauty pageant she had just won.

The spirit of small-town Michigan is visible in the zestful glee of its younger residents.

In small towns, youngsters often have to make their own entertainment. Many play softball and are Little Leaguers. Hanging out or cruising on Main Street occupies many teenagers on weekend nights. The local fishing hole is a popular spot on summer mornings.

Main Street would not be the same if there weren't kids riding bikes, milling around or inventing games. Whether it's hanging out at the corner grocery store or playing softball on the town's only diamond, small-town kids have a brand of activity all their own.

Dansville

Laura Yenz gets her pony, Snowflake, ready for the youngster's first ride in the Dansville Memorial Day parade.

Eighth-grader Jimmy Nagy, 14, far left, helps his fourth-grade brother, Jesse, 8, with his English assignment in the one-room school on Bois Blanc Island. Left, the brothers ride their four-wheel-drive vehicle to school. Below, teacher Geri Malenfant leads her only two students in the Pledge of Allegiance.

Malenfant, 25, helps Jesse as Jimmy watches. Right, she stands in the doorway with the entire student population.

Bois Blanc Is.

Pines School District No. 1 teacher Geri Malenfant should have little trouble remembering the names of her students.

Fourth-grader Jesse Nagy and his eighth-grade brother, Jimmy, were the only students in the 1984-85 school year in the tiny school on Bois Blanc Island near Mackinac Island.

The one-room school is Michigan's smallest, and its costliest per student. With an annual budget of $30,000, Jimmy and Jesse get $15,000 worth of education each.

In fact, there are more people on the five-member school board than in the school itself. The island's population is only 50.

Getting to the school is half the fun for Jesse and Jimmy. Every school day, they get on their four-wheel-drive vehicle for the four-mile drive to school. In the winter, they use their snowmobiles.

The teacher-student ratio has been beneficial, especially for Jimmy. "I was having a lot of trouble in a regular school," he said. "Up here you get a better education."

First-grader Kenny Wnadahsega spends his recess sitting on the lawn in front of the Hannahville Indian School in the Upper Peninsula. Above, third-grader Heather Teeple does some homework during lunch hour.

The first high school graduation ceremony at the Nah Tah Wahsh (Hannahville Indian School) was a community event. Everybody came: Relatives, tribal leaders, the media and even a couple of state school board members and Michigan Department of Education officials.

"This is really a celebration for Indians across Michigan because a lot of (Indian) people from all over the state send kids here to school," said Joan Webkamigad, an Indian consultant on bilingual and migrant education for the state.

The 1984 ceremony highlighted a nine-year effort to better educate people who live on the Hannahville Indian Reservation. The school was built by the Potawatomi, and includes kindergarten through 12th grades. Ninety percent of the school-age children on the reservation attend the school.

After the graduation festivities, one of the four graduates, Ruth Meshiguad, still wiping tears, said: "I'm really happy. I'm happy for everyone else, besides myself.

"I feel fulfilled. I've reached one goal. Now I can go on to another one."

Hannahville

A bus brings students home on the Hannahville Indian Reservation, above. Right, bus driver Jerome McCullough talks with Rachel Compo as they wait for other students to board the bus. Far right, second-grader Gina Shawano works on her penmanship. The sign above her says "blackboard" in Ojibwa.

Tammy Meshigaud shares her lilacs with Jessica Eichhorn, left, and Loretta Wandahsega. Younger students were outside for recess while older students stayed inside. Far right, recess is a good time to catch up on some reading as first-grade teacher Tom Kennedy helps Richard Sagataw with his alphabet book and Stephanie Meshigaud looks on.

Matt Lutz stands in the family barn.

Sebewaing

In the middle of tough times for the farming industry, teenager Matt Lutz is committed to being a farmer.

"I wanted to be a farmer all my life," said the student at Unionville Sebewaing High School. "Farmers take pride in what they are doing. They are living their work and not just working."

When asked about the economics of farming, Lutz said, "I think when the times are tough, that's a test of what you are."

Lutz helps with chores on the 120-acre family farm in Sebewaing. Every morning and evening he feeds 250 hogs. He also helps his father, uncle and grandfather during the planting and harvest seasons.

"I would like to keep the farm in the family," said Lutz.

"My dad thinks it's a good idea, but he won't hold me back if I want to do something else."

The younger Lutz also is a member of his high school's chapter of Future Farmers of America.

Lutz spends his spare time with friends — most of whom also want to be farmers — and his girlfriend, Sandy Singer. "She is not from a farm family, but she says she wants to come over and see what I do on the farm," said Lutz.

"After graduation, I might go to college or look for a job and save money to buy a farm."

Lutz looks out from the barn while doing his chores after school. Left, he feeds some of his family's more than 250 hogs.

Lutz helps his girlfriend, Sandy Singer, study for a test before classes. Lutz and Singer eat a late dinner at a fast-food restaurant. They drove to Bay City to see a movie.

It's a doubleheader for these two Little League teams in Hillman. Five Little League teams play in the Hillman league, a town of about 850. At bottom, shortstop Trapper Linseman gnaws at his mitt during the game against Frye Forest Products.

The dusty infield of Hillman's Tripp Field is a far cry from the manicured grass at Tiger Stadium, but the game is just as important for these small-town Little Leaguers.

Youngsters in Hillman, as in many small towns, get a solid sports background. In this town of 500 people, there are five Little League teams, five Pee Wee League teams and several Pony League and girls softball teams. "When school is out for the summer, these are the only organized activities for the kids," says Mike Bowden, who is in charge of the leagues.

The Little League teams are formed in a random draft with players' names arbitrarily divided up and assigned to teams.

"We have seven new rookies on this team," says Kenyon Construction coach Jack Linseman. "But we have fun."

Trapper Linseman and his teammates on the Kenyon Construction team cheer on their team, above. Kenyon Construction left fielder Charlie Davis serves as first-base coach, left.

Hillman

Coach Jack Linseman gives Dave Hornbacher a pep talk, right. Hornbacher, a substitute, was hit by a pitch the last time he was at bat. Below, team members from Frye Forest Products and Kenyon Construction shake hands after Frye won, 12-3. Far right, after the game, Little Leaguers enjoy ice cream and verbal replays of the game as they walk in downtown Hillman.

Bridgman

Bridgman is a basketball town.

The high school boys Class D team has been the talk of the town since their first state championship in the 1920s.

The 1986 team also kept this southwest Michigan town in basketball fever. It closed the regular season with a 57-55 victory over Eau Claire High School that sent the more than 2,000 spectators — a figure close to Bridgman's population — into a frenzy.

The win was the team's 20th of the year and closed its first undefeated regular season since Bridgman last won the state championship 40 years ago.

The Bridgman team heads out of the locker room to a cheering crowd for the last regular season game, far left. Signs of inspiration are all over the locker room. Above, senior Brett Germain is introduced before his last home game. At left, more than 2,000 fans fill the gymnasium to see the Bees play.

Center Jamie VanShaardenberg shoots over Saugatuck defenders in a regular season game. Right, players embrace after a 57-55 victory over Eau Claire, which gave the team a 20-0 regular season. The team lost in regional competition.

138

Minutes after 18-year-old high school senior Christine Rigozzi was crowned Miss Bangor 1986, someone in the audience said, "I could say that was my barber's daughter."

During her radio interview after winning the title, the new Miss Bangor, who represents the southwestern Michigan town of 2,100, was worried about telling her boss that she couldn't cook Sunday at the Bangor Freeze because of her new duties.

The annual Bangor beauty pageant is a part of life in the town. "The beauty pageant is one of the highlights for Bangor," said Darlene Seymoure of the queen's committee.

On contest night, it was standing room only as 1,000 people filled the elementary school auditorium.

The pageant also attracted some past queens, including 72-year-old Ruby Rackie, Miss Bangor 1932.

The 17 contestants were all Bangor High School students. All but two were seniors and most had had relatives or friends in past pageants.

"I have been coming here every year since I was eight years old," Rigozzi said. "I loved the beautiful gowns and the astonishment of the girls that won."

Laurie Bauck remembered seeing her mother's pageant gown. Her aunt also was in the pageant.

A young girl, top left, looks at stars with pictures of the other queens from nearby towns who were to compete for the title of Miss Blossomtime. Above, Chris Nozicka does a last-minute touch-up of Christine Rigozzi's hair while other contestants watch. Left, Laura Marters hugs finalist Crystal Carr in the girls' locker room. On the next page, the three finalists, from left, Rigozzi, Shawn Burlingham and Carr, anxiously await the decision from the judges. Rigozzi won, Burlingham was first runner-up and Carr was second runner-up.

Bangor

And the winner is . . . Christine Rigozzi. Right, Miss Bangor 1986 and her family after the pageant.

Marion

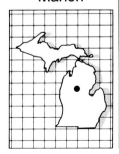

On the preceding pages, teenagers hang out downtown on a summer day in Marion, a town of 1,500.

Sebewaing

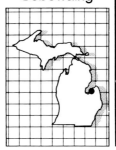

A typical Saturday night in Sebewaing for teenagers includes a packed pickup truck cruising downtown and hanging out at the Shell station to talk to friends and to find out where parties are.

Trenary

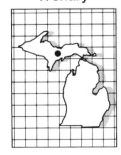

Betty Cayer smiles during a break in her job making lunches for the students at Mathies Township School in Trenary in the Upper Peninsula. She has cooked for about 4,000 students in her 20 years on the job.

Manistique

Triplets are a lot of babies for any couple to handle, and Michigan's first set of test-tube triplets, in Manistique, are no exception. Taking care of John Earl, Angela Marie, and Ryan Francis, are mom, Sharon Burns; dad, George Burns, and grandmother, Pat Roddy.

Saline

A 4-H participant and her calf wear matching bonnets during a Saline fair.

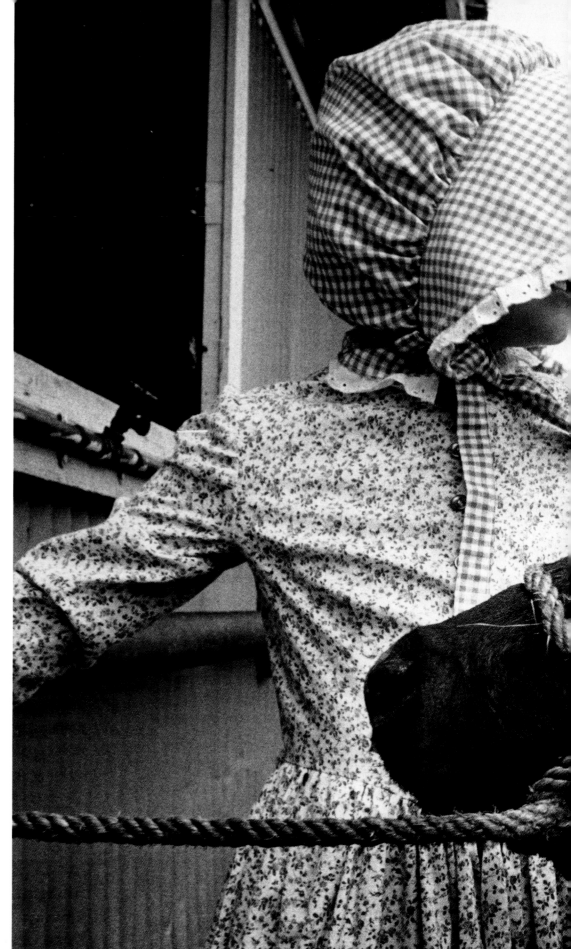

Moran

These young hunters from the town of Moran show off their kill. From left are Donny Orr, 17; Richie Sayles, 16, and Ed Wilk, 15.

Leoni Township

Hanging out at Digger's Grocery Store in Leoni Township outside Jackson are Derek O'Dell, Amanda O'Dell and Matthew Burrow. The owners of the store are Linda and Donald (Digger) O'Dell; Derek is their son and Amanda and Matthew are their grandchildren.

Dollar Bay

Three-month-old Kelly Nye gets a sled ride in Dollar Bay, a town of about 800.

Celebrations

"This weekend is one of the biggest events in this town. Everybody shares and helps. It is the little town with the big heart."
— Dansville village President Clayton Johnson Jr. on the town's Memorial Day parade.

It doesn't take long to find some sort of celebration or festival around Michigan. There's the annual Tulip Festival in Holland, the Cherry Festival in Traverse City and the Maple Syrup Festival in Vermontville.

In small towns, celebrations aren't taken lightly. The festivities take on the spirit of the small towns and the volunteers who make them possible.

In many towns, the events have become part of the town's identity.

Many of the happenings occur annually and are a time to work with neighbors, trade bits of gossip about family and friends and enjoy reunions with people who have left but never quite given up their small-town roots.

Vermontville

The carnival rides are a big attraction during the weekend-long Maple Syrup Festival in Vermontville.

The Dansville Aggies marching band leaves Fairview Cemetery after memorial services, above. Sarah Hardin, 3, right, waves to the Dansville Agricultural School alumni band from her front lawn. Above right, members of the Veterans of Foreign Wars Auxiliary watch the ceremony at the cemetery.

The rain clouds didn't deter the crowd that came to see what Dansville folks called "one of the best parades in central Michigan."

And as the parade headed onto M-36 and the heart of town, the crowd of about 2,000 cheered. There were about four times as many parade-goers as the entire population of 480.

The parade was part of a weekend celebration that included bingo, a barn dance, a chicken barbecue and hot-air balloon rides.

"This weekend is one of the biggest events in this town," said village President Clayton Johnson Jr. "Everybody shares and helps. It is the little town with the big heart."

With the Dansville Aggies marching band leading the way, the parade headed to the Fairview Cemetery for memorial services. After the services, the parade reassembled and headed back toward the center of town for an encore.

Dansville

Townspeople line the banks of the South Branch of the Au Sable River to watch the centennial raft race, above. Far left, Clayton and Doloris Burrows are Roscommon's king and queen for the centennial parade. The retired couple was nominated by the people at the Roscommon Senior Center. They are in front of a 1925 Rolls-Royce. Middle left, Huck Finn, alias Mike Pflun, watches the parade at Wallace Park. From left, Faye Swatz, Marie Marsh, Salome Sheppard and Huttie Kenyon wear period costumes to celebrate Roscommon's 100th birthday, left.

Several French Marines gather around the campfire, above. Paul Beauvais, right, stands guard over his family's tepee outside Fort Michilimackinac after the annual pageant recreating events from 1715 to 1781. Beauvais was one of 30 French Marines in period costumes who took part in the pageant. Middle, Beauvais, wife Patricia and daughter Michele break down their tepee after three days. Far right, after the Memorial weekend pageant, the family breaks for ice cream.

The Mackinac Bridge looms in the background behind Fort Michilimackinac, a historical landmark in Mackinaw City.

Participants in the Fort Michilimackinac Pageant head out the front of the fort to re-enact early American and Michigan history. The 250 people take part in one of the oldest and most colorful historical pageants in the nation.

A boy in British period clothing gets a good view of the pageant from above.

On the next page, three girls take a peek through the logs to get a view of the historical re-enactment while awaiting their turns to participate.

Some of the more than 100 volunteers show their working tools during a break in the work on the house, far left. Owner Judy Hicks, above, strips old paint from a door while her husband, Gary, eats cold pizza for dinner. Retiree Fred Dickenson paints the door frame, below.

It was a community project with a lot of work, sweat and fun. Volunteers with the Tecumseh Area Historical Society restored a 19th-Century home for the town's home tour.

About 100 volunteers put in long hours to help restore the Bacon-Cairns House, built during the 1860s, for the tour, part of the Promenade the Past celebration.

The home went through a year of extensive restoration to bring back its original Greek Revival architecture and an Italianate addition.

The house has been reopened as a bed-and-breakfast place, the Boulevard Inn.

Tecumseh

171

Marian Stafford stencils a Victorian pattern on the stairs while Joyce Ramsey-Grier paints. Right, window painter Bob Doeri gets some help from sons Adrian and Pierce.

Bliss

A procession leaves the Bliss Pioneer Memorial Church for the cemetery after the 98th annual Memorial Day services. The short parade was led by veterans groups from neighboring towns. Above, Susannah Dankert places flowers on graves.

More than 100 Danish-Americans over the age of 40 spend the first and third Friday nights of each month doing variations of the square dance, round dance and other Danish dances in the 135-year-old Trufant Community Building.

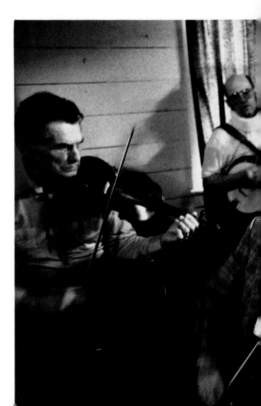

Four dancers take a break. The dance has been held for seven years in the predominantly Danish town of 600.

Above, couples round dance at the Old Timers dance in Trufant. The Frank Mattison Orchestra, left, has been performing there for seven years.

Trufant

Colon

Jerry Conklin suspends assistant Paula Underwood under Colon's one blinking traffic light, surrounded by magicians from the town. The resort town of 1,000 has been dubbed the Magic Capital of the World. There is a lot of magic about Colon, says Greg Bordner, owner of Abbott's Magic Co., a magic supply store.

The tradition lives on

"My dad bought the bar in 1914, and I was born upstairs. I grew up in this bar, and I have been here ever since, other than a couple of years in the Navy. — Bernie Shute, owner of Shute's 1890 Bar in Calumet.

I have had this romantic notion that there is a piece of Americana out there in its own special time warp.

That there are people and things still living in a previous era — towns that have not yet seen the neon lights.

I have found people and places that recall such an era, and have relished their special strengths. I reached for my camera quickly, somehow fearing that they would quickly modernize.

They didn't and the results have been some of my favorite pictures.

I felt privileged to have experienced this special time machine.

near Potterville 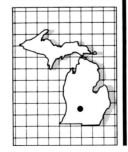 An antique car heading home from a parade passes the West Benton United Methodist Church, just outside Potterville.

Cedar
Ludington
Parnell

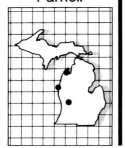

The sun shines through the Marquette Memorial Cross that overlooks Lake Michigan in Ludington, right. The Holy Rosary Catholic Church in Cedar is part of the winter landscape in the Grand Traverse Bay area, below. The average annual snowfall in the area is 84.6 inches, according to the National Weather Service office in Muskegon. Far right, St. Patrick's Catholic Church is framed between old tombstones in the adjacent cemetery in the town of Parnell.

Calvin Hill, far left, seems lost in his own world during Sunday school in Idlewild. Congregation members gather to talk after services, above. Below, usher Fannie Shelton talks with choir member Demitra Holmes, 8, before services begin. On the next pages, congregation members kneel during prayer service near the altar.

Idlewild

185

Church usher Ada Mae Day has been helping churchgoers at Tabernacle African Methodist Episcopal Church in Idlewild for 30 years.

"There has been a lot of changes," said Day. "Kids grow up, get married and go away."

The church is in the middle of this black resort retirement community with 850 year-round residents.

The services have a small-town pace. Five children make up the Sunday school services.

After church, the congregation gathers to share the week's stories and talk of upcoming events in the community.

Clarence Johnson, a longtime resident of Idlewild, prepares his music before joining the choir procession to start services, left. Pastor J.H. Kittrewl preaches at the pulpit, top. From left, Anton Hill, Pete Brown and Calvin Hill, show varied reactions to Sunday school lessons.

Wide-brimmed hats, homemade clothes and quilts made powerful in simplicity and color.

The Amish.

Although most of America's "plain people" are settled in Pennsylvania, there are several areas of Michigan where Amish black horse-drawn buggies are prevalent.

The Amish faith — officially known as the Old Order Amish Mennonite Church — is named for Jacob Amman,

An Amish family heads home with their horse and buggy after doing business in Clare, at top. Above, an Amish farmer and his son head back to the barn with their wagon. Two Amish women bring in groceries from their buggy after shopping in Clare, above right. Young Amish children play on the lawn of their home in Fairview, bottom right.

who led the split from the Mennonite Church in the 1690s. The Amish began migrating to North America from Europe in the 1700s.

Their religion stresses that separation from the world is a way to be closer to God. The Amish express that clearly in their cultural non-conformity.

There are about 82,000 members of the Old Order of the Amish Church in the United States.

Cornstalks stacked by hand form a pattern in a snow-covered field outside Centreville. Right, an Amish boy carries water to a tilling farmer in Fairview.

The interior of Shute's bar is reminiscent of the early 1900s. Owner Bernie Shute cleans every night after closing and before opening on Sundays to keep up the decor.

Calumet

The story of Shute's 1890 Bar in Calumet, a former copper mining town, is the story of 59-year-old Bernie Shute.

"My dad bought the bar in 1914, and I was born upstairs," said Shute. "I grew up in this bar, and have been here ever since, other than a couple of years in the Navy."

Little has changed in the bar since Shute's father bought it. It is one of 10 bars in a town that at the turn of the century, the height of the copper mining boom, had more churches and bars per capita than any other city in the country.

The bar is like home for Shute. "I always work alone," said Shute. He works about 105 hours each week tending bar and polishing the bar's woodwork.

"You know, bar life is not the worst of lives, but it's not the best of lives, either," Shute said. "You just make the best of it."

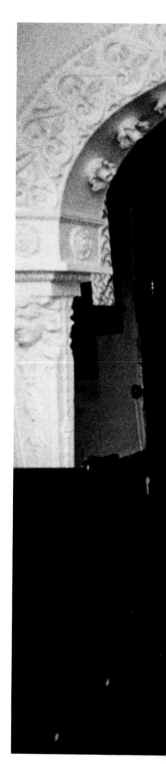

Bernie Shute reads near the door for better light. The bar owner also has been the Calumet village fire chief for the last 30 years.

Ovid McDonald spends a cold winter afternoon warming up. Below, Shute joins McDonald on the bar stools, leaving his worn-out chair behind the bar.

Mackinac Island

A horse-drawn wagon with driver and two dogs heads to the dock on Mackinac Island to pick up construction material. Main Street was dug up to install a new water system and to bury telephone and electrical lines. The street was repaved in time for the annual onslaught of summer tourists.

Negaunee

In a contrast between the old and the new, the Negaunee Mall frames the Breitung Hotel, which closed last summer. When the mining industry was booming around the turn of the century, the hotel overlooked a long row of thriving businesses. Today the hotel is closed, the business district is a few blocks shorter and some of the old businesses are closed. But the hotel now overlooks the new mall, opened in 1985, that is the hope for Negaunee's downtown.

Sebewaing

Roger Sy, left, and Joe Zalesky spend their break time looking out the window of Sebewaing Industries, a metal stamping plant. The Statue of Liberty painting was done in 1976 in memory of an area high school student killed in an auto accident.

ONE NATION, UNDER GOD...

Michigan's Main Streets

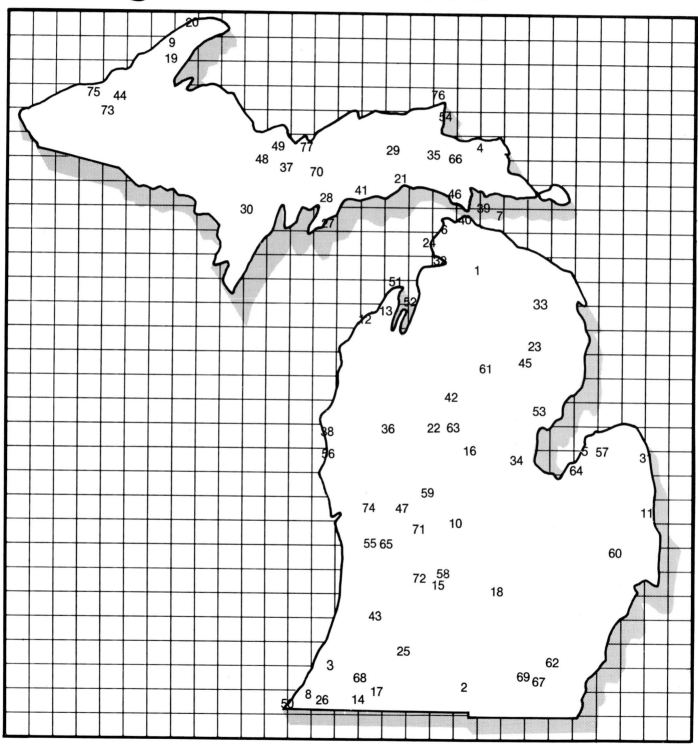

Index